IMAGES
of America

KNOXVILLE IN THE VIETNAM ERA

ON THE COVER: This is an image of c. 1963 downtown Knoxville from the civil rights collection at the Beck Cultural Exchange Center. Policemen were on duty primarily to thwart troublemakers, but they also arrested protesters who refused to obey a command. Sometimes 50 or more people were arrested at a time. (Courtesy of the Beck Cultural Exchange Center and Knoxville *News Sentinel*.)

IMAGES
of America

KNOXVILLE IN THE VIETNAM ERA

Ed Hooper

ARCADIA PUBLISHING

ISBN 978-0-7385-5341-2

Published by Arcadia Publishing
Charleston SC, Chicago IL, Portsmouth NH, San Francisco CA

Printed in the United States of America

Library of Congress Catalog Card Number: 2007936490

For all general information contact Arcadia Publishing at:
Telephone 843-853-2070
Fax 843-853-0044
E-mail sales@arcadiapublishing.com
For customer service and orders:
Toll-Free 1-888-313-2665

Visit us on the Internet at www.arcadiapublishing.com

This book is dedicated to the memory of James "Buddy" White and to the men and women of Knoxville and East Tennessee who so valiantly served in the Vietnam War.

Contents

ACKNOWLEDGMENTS

I would like to acknowledge the following people, businesses, and organizations for their assistance in acquiring these photographs: F. A. Blankenship; publisher Bruce Hartmann and Jack McElroy of the Knoxville *News Sentinel*; Col. Ron Borden and Ranger Cadet Jesse Ryan at the University of Tennessee Army ROTC Program; Jefferson Chapman and the McClung Museum; Avon Rollins and Sue Ann Reece of the Beck Cultural Exchange Center; Cynthia Tinker at the University of Tennessee Center for the Study of War and Society; Fred Reagan; Kathy Jones; Sen. Tim Burchett; Sen. Jamie Woodson; and the command staff of the Tennessee National Guard.

Introduction

The years from 1961 to 1975 were a complicated stretch of time where everything seemed to change in Knoxville. A booming economy, the Tennessee Valley Authority's hydroelectric dam projects, and the continued development of Oak Ridge increased Knoxville's population tremendously, and social issues dominated current events.

In the forefront of it all, however, was the ongoing conflict in Southeast Asia and a war unlike any other. The headlines and analysis of newspapers in wars past gave way to the immediacy of television, and the Vietnam War became one fought in living rooms across the nation. With Americans two generations away from World War II, people who could never imagine the horrors of war suddenly viewed it in living color from the comfort of their own homes, and the effect was unpredictably powerful.

The government contractors headquartered in Knoxville and the longstanding military tradition of East Tennessee made the region a vital resource of products and personnel to the U.S. military. The city center, which had been creeping westward for a generation, suddenly stopped crawling and started racing west as interstates eased passage into Oak Ridge and to the supporting industries that sprang up to service the government village.

Longtime family farms gave way to subdivisions, and while hundreds of homes were filling the gaps between the city and Oak Ridge, a period of urban decay was launched in the once-pristine downtown section of Knoxville. With the opening of West Town Mall in 1972, a new way of shopping was born, and the busy streets of downtown Knoxville started falling silent for the first time in more than 100 years.

Small businesses and family dwellings began disappearing, and the city found itself economically anchoring to the Tennessee Valley Authority (TVA), the University of Tennessee, Knoxville (UT), and government offices—fighting to keep the downtown section alive and prevent "brown fields" from overtaking what was once the industrial heartbeat of the Tennessee Valley. West Knox County suddenly became the fastest growing section in the region. From Papermill Road to Cedar Bluff, new business and industries starting springing up and the population in the area boomed.

The epic of the Vietnam War was always in the forefront of the American psyche, but it has to be remembered there were only three television networks and a handful of radio stations with news departments. Newscasts were short and information about the war in Vietnam limited. Social issues at home were the dominant conversation and competed for newscasts and ink space, not to mention the ongoing cold war between the United States and the USSR, Communism's appearance on the United States' doorstep in Latin America, and an anti-military movement that was in full force stateside, spurring distrust of the U.S. armed forces.

The distrust of the military found a home on college campuses across the nation and in East Tennessee. It became an attitude that bled into everyday society, and when the war ended, those men and women became the first American soldiers to return home from a war front with no victory celebrations, no ticker tape, not even a "welcome home." There were no heroes in their ranks as far as anyone was concerned. In fact, many of the soldiers were spit upon, accused of crimes they did not commit, and stripped of the pride and honor befitting a returning warrior. Those who had dodged the war, fled to Canada, or outright refused to go, however, were deemed heroes by the new standards. Yet the men and women who courageously served in Vietnam defined an entire generation of Americans and for good reason. More than three million people served in the Vietnam War, the United States spent $120 billion to fight it, and the casualty rate during that time period was incredible. More than 58,000 soldiers were killed, 2,000 went missing, and 300,000 were wounded.

There were so many great stories and discoveries that fell through the cracks of the nation in the Vietnam era, especially here in East Tennessee. This is a sample of those stories.

One

Above Top Secret

James Thomas (Tom) Davis was your stereotypical East Tennessean who spent his time growing up hunting and fishing. With the Big South Fork as a playground, Davis was never far from his rifle or fishing rod throughout his youth, and when not working at his father's drugstore, you could find him prowling in the rolling hills.

He went to Tennessee Technological University in Cookeville and married his high school sweetheart, and the couple worked to build a home. In 1959, with a year to go in college, Davis and his brother both quit school to join the U.S. Army under the "buddy system" that allowed them to go through basic training together.

After training at Fort Jackson, Tom Davis was transferred by U.S. Army Intelligence and Security Command to Fort Devens, Massachusetts, where he trained in the classified Radio Directions Finders course. Upon completion, Davis was sent to the U.S. Army Security Agency Instructors Training Course, which was under the operational guidance of the National Security Agency, and trained for another year.

On May 5, 1961, Davis was issued orders to report to Saigon, Vietnam. He packed up his belongings, sent his wife and seven-month-old daughter, Cindy, back to their home in Livingston and shipped out to Vietnam where he joined the 3rd Radio Research Unit (RRU) as part of the Military Advisory Group. His assignment was to train South Vietnamese troops in communications intelligence and help them locate Viet Cong and North Vietnamese radio transmitters.

On December 22, Davis and 10 soldiers from the Army of the Republic of Vietnam (ARVN) were assigned to monitor a suspected North Vietnamese unit and begin sweeping for their signals. While doing so, the unit came under attack, and Specialist 4th Class (Sp4c.) James Thomas Davis was killed.

This was the beginning of the Vietnam War for Tennesseans. In a speech years later, Pres. Lyndon B. Johnson identified Davis as the first American GI to be killed in combat in Vietnam.

Details of Davis's death remained classified for more than a generation. This is the first time the Davis family has granted permission for these photographs to be seen outside the family circle.

This is the standard army photograph most people have seen of Sp4c. James Thomas Davis. Because of the nature and sensitivity of his assignment with the Army Security Agency, little information was ever revealed about his work. (Courtesy of Bill, Joe, Janie, and Jack Davis.)

Davis is pictured here in Vietnam with his then-classified mobile radio detection equipment. The Army Security Agency used these devices to locate enemy cross talk that would give them directions to the enemy's camps and aid in discovering their movements in the region. Davis (below) had a stellar reputation among his men and the 3rd RRU with whom he had completed numerous successful missions by locating enemy forces. (Courtesy of Bill, Joe, Janie, and Jack Davis.)

As an advisor with the Army Security Agency's 3rd Radio Research Unit, Specialist 4 Davis did not serve in what is commonly thought of as a "company" of U.S. soldiers. He worked with the South Vietnamese Army as one of their members. It meant he immersed himself in local culture and learned everything he could about their lives and habits. In a letter home to his father, he

wrote, "I am seeing as much and as many things as possible, Dad. It is really an experience for me. The country is very beautiful and the people fascinating. I believe I have really learned a lot since coming here." Here Davis is pictured enjoying a meal with the ARVN soldiers he trained and worked with in Vietnam. (Courtesy of Bill, Joe, Janie, and Jack Davis.)

This is a picture of Davis with his ARVN unit outside the barracks near Saigon. This photograph is a good illustration of the military advisor relationship with the South Vietnamese Army. The advisors helped with tactics, intelligence, and some operations, but the bulk of the work fell to the ARVN to do. (Courtesy of Bill, Joe, Janie, and Jack Davis.)

Davis took this photograph of a group of Vietnamese children outside the gate of a military compound. The children would often gather outside military compounds to get candy and food from the troops. Many were orphaned, deserted, or lost, as hostilities would often separate families. The soldiers were sometimes the only family the children had. (Courtesy of Bill, Joe, Janie, and Jack Davis.)

This is a field unit of ARVN troops working with Davis and the Army Security Agency's 3rd Radio Research Unit. The relationship between Davis and the men he trained in the field was close, and between missions, he found time to relax and take pictures to send home. (Courtesy of Bill, Joe, Janie, and Jack Davis.)

This is a troop transport truck like the one Davis was traveling in when his 10-man squad came under attack. The North Vietnamese reportedly detonated an explosive device, and the ARVN unit with Davis was ambushed by the guerillas. Davis, who was said to be riding as a passenger, pushed one of his officers clear of the vehicle and made it to the ditch, where he began firing his weapon to cover his officer's escape. In the firefight that followed, Davis was struck by enemy fire and killed. (Courtesy of Bill, Joe, Janie, and Jack Davis.)

This is Tom Davis (left) with an ARVN officer near Saigon. Following the incident that resulted in Davis's death, the men in the 3rd RRU and the South Vietnamese command were devastated by his death. In a letter to the Davis family in Tennessee, South Vietnamese Lt. Col. Vo Dai Khoi, chief signal officer, wrote; "Mr. Davis had come and lived among us with most intrepid compassion for our cause and a most amiable friend. Together we have enjoyed our friendship, which fostered the most praise-worthy espirit de corps ever encountered between soldiers of different nations. With born noble gestures, he had behaved himself admirably and qualified himself as a model soldier endowed with a rare personality." (Courtesy of Bill, Joe, Janie, and Jack Davis.)

Following Davis being killed in action, the members of the 3rd Radio Research Unit knew the Tennessee soldier would not be acknowledged because of the national security issues surrounding their work. The men worked nonstop for 24 hours making a beaded funeral pall that draped his coffin, which is now in the Tennessee State Museum. The 3rd RRU cantonment area pictured here was named in honor of Sp4c. James Thomas Davis. The photograph at right is of the headquarters building at Davis Station. (Above courtesy of Rick Merz; right courtesy of the National Security Agency.)

Cryptologist Sp4c. James Thomas Davis's body was sent to Clark Air Base, Philippines, where he was routed to his home in Livingston, Tennessee. On January 4, 1962, Overton County native Tom Davis was buried with full military honors in Good Hope Cemetery in Livingston. Davis's service would eventually be honored by the state of Tennessee and the nation when Pres. Lyndon B. Johnson identified him as the first combat casualty of the Vietnam War. (Courtesy of Bill, Joe, Janie, and Jack Davis.)

Davis was one of hundreds of U.S. cryptologists killed in action and never publicly recognized for the scope of their service to the nation. The National Security Agency erected this monument bearing the names of American servicemen and women who have given their lives in often-classified operations. (Courtesy of the National Security Agency.)

Two

A City in Flux

The news of Tom Davis's death was carried in the Knoxville newspapers and on local broadcasts, but no one truly understood the impact his death would have on the Tennessee Valley. Vietnam was not a "call to action" like the city had seen in World War I and World War II. It was a back-page war fought much like the Korean War with the 17th Parallel in Vietnam replacing the 38th in Korea. It was often forgotten in the news as other issues dominated the headlines and the city grappled with trying to hold on to its identity.

The city was still growing in the early 1960s, and Gay Street was still the center of the city. Much of the outlying area was still working family farms and rural areas, but the new interstates that came through the city brought with them a change of attitude, especially among the younger generation who discovered they could make more money selling the family farms to contractors and developers building homes to accommodate those leaving downtown Knoxville and moving west to the country.

Urban planning and renewal were relatively new concepts in the city as officials tried to find a way to keep interest in downtown. Aging buildings and warehouses were slowly being deserted, and new ideas to preserve them were few and far between, especially as the economy began to shift from agriculture to industry. The once-busy Market House off of Gay Street was falling silent, and the stalls that sold everything imaginable were barely finding enough tenants to keep them in business.

Knoxville tried to adapt and reworked highways to develop an industry-friendly city. To some extent, the changes were successful, but aging infrastructure has its own way of halting progress, and there is only so much that a government can do to revitalize a city. It worked at first, but they could not stem the flow of people from the city to the country where taxes were cheaper and land easily available.

This is an aerial view of Baxter Avenue around 1963. The cloverleaf exchange was built in hopes that this region of the city would attract new industry and service existing industries there. Although numerous small businesses were established in the area, no major industries ever located there.

At one time, this was the far reaches of west Knox County. This picturesque farmland and rolling countryside is the Cedar Bluff interchange in the early 1960s. It is easy to note that there was not even a single gas station at the location when this photograph was taken.

This desolate piece of countryside is Mabry Hood Road. Like Cedar Bluff, it was primarily farmland and rural homes. This is today a heavily populated and vibrant part of the city's business community.

This is a photograph from the same era of Papermill Road. On the right, note there is some subdivision development. It was regarded in the 1960s as extreme West Knoxville. Today this is the geographic center of the city in terms of population and area.

This was one of the last photographs of a bustling Gay Street in 1966. Stores, restaurants, and theaters were still major draws downtown for residents. This was taken prior to a parade downtown. By the mid-1970s, the busy downtown section had fallen on hard times. The prestigious Bijou Theater at the far end of Gay Street in the old Lamar Hotel, which counted U.S. presidents among its guests over the years, became an adult movie house before the revitalization of the 1980s.

The absence of streetcars and suitable mass transit for downtown chipped away at the numbers of people who traveled to Gay Street on a daily basis to shop. This is the back side of Gay Street's Promenade where major department stores were located in the city. Featured in the lower left is the once-popular Blue Circle restaurant, whose 12¢ hamburgers became a mainstay among teenagers in East Tennessee. Only one store of the popular chain remains in the upper East Tennessee city of Kingsport.

This is an image looking south at the Gay Street Bridge from the Knoxville waterfront on the Tennessee River. While dotted with community parks, restaurants, and shops today, the once-industrial riverfront was never seriously looked upon in the 1960s as a part of a popular downtown development plan.

The Promenade off of Gay Street also doubled as an events location for the city where car, boat, and art shows were often held. The downward slope of the land running parallel to Gay Street was hoped to provide easier access to a residential base that moved from streetcars to single automobiles. Below is a view of the parking behind the Promenade. Parking lots downtown went from offering full service to automobiles—oil changes, car washes, and general maintenance—to just parking places for automobiles. Because city and state offices were located downtown, parking and traffic from Knox County and surrounding areas to downtown Knoxville became a major issue and is still cited as one of the most popular reasons for people to avoid the city.

In an attempt to attract people to the experience of shopping in downtown Knoxville, the city erected these mushroom-like caps to shield pedestrians from the weather. It dramatically changed the look of Market Square, which was regarded by many residents as the heart of the city. The appearance of the sidewalk "caps" detracted from the architecture of downtown and, for many residents, was the low point of downtown development. Below is a better look at how the modern design took away from the pristine center of Knoxville. Today the square has returned to its pre-1960 appearance and is again regarded as a centerpiece of Knoxville's downtown.

This is a photograph of the locally popular Rich's Department Store located downtown. The department store was regarded as one of the best in Knoxville and was described as full-service—featuring an inside restaurant and home furnishings.

This structure built on the University of Tennessee campus in 1969 is probably the most significant and influential building constructed during the Vietnam era. The Clarence Brown Theater is named after UT alumnus and film director Clarence Brown. While it is regarded as one of the most respected theaters in the Southeast, this is also where thousands of schoolchildren across East Tennessee get their first exposure to the performing arts. The 576-seat theater features internationally known guest artists, plays, and dance performances and has served as the centerpiece of not only the university, but also county school systems across the region.

Three

THE WAR AT HOME

Like most American cities, the social issues in Knoxville often dominated the headlines and news broadcasts of the 1960s, pushing the war in Vietnam to the back burner. One of the most vibrant issues of the day was the civil rights movement, and the city was a hotbed for it. With the Highlander Center (a training center for civil rights protestors) nearby, many of the civil rights pioneers were trained in East Tennessee to lead the peaceful, albeit loud, protests that grabbed the nation's attention and made Americans ask the hard questions of race and privilege in everyday society.

Since the disastrous 1896 *Plessy v. Ferguson* ruling by the U.S. Supreme Court, "separate, but equal" was the law of the land. Both black and white existed in the same country under the same Constitution but in two different worlds. There was a working class, a middle class, and an upper class for both black and white citizens—each with their own traditional sections of towns and businesses and events where black and white were officially separated.

Supreme Court reversals started happening through peaceful protests that led to court actions overturning the Victorian judgment on a national level, but changing laws on a state and local level took far more effort. U.S. citizens seeking a society where all were equal took to the streets and forced local governments and state legislatures to repeal statutes that told them with whom they could associate, eat, drink, or live. By the Vietnam era, this had become a nationwide movement that involved Americans—black and white—from all walks of life.

Knoxville was no different. Civil rights marches took place in the very heart of downtown and filled the newspapers and news broadcasts of the day. Day and night, Knoxville's black residents and others who sided with them marched against theaters, diners, and department stores. It was through the lenses of the Knoxville *News Sentinel* and their reporters that this period in American history was documented, and with their assistance and Avon Rollins of the Beck Cultural Exchange Center, we are able to remember and commemorate the efforts of those who made equal rights for everyone a part of American society.

Knoxvillian Robert Booker (left) talks to John Bell in 1961. Booker and Bell, dean of men at Knoxville College, converse through the city jail peep slot. Booker was arrested at the Tennessee Theater on October 9, 1961. He would go on to serve a term as a state legislator and become a respected columnist and historian. (Courtesy of Knoxville *News Sentinel* and Beck Cultural Exchange Center.)

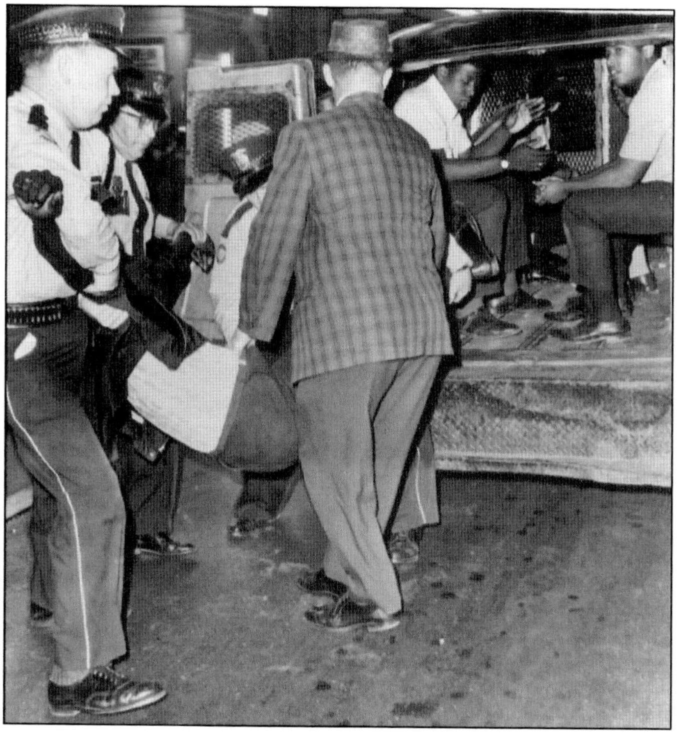

Knoxville College students are being led to the city jail. Jerry Porter (center), one of the student leaders, claps his hands in support as fellow students are taken to jail. Knoxville College, which was the city's traditional black college, served as a hotbed of civil rights activities during the 1960s. (Courtesy of Knoxville *News Sentinel* and Beck Cultural Exchange Center.)

The arrest of William Marvin Gordon Jr. in the early 1960s created a stir when it reached the newspapers. His father, W. M. Gordon Sr., was a city police officer who often drove the paddy wagon that took his son to jail. (Courtesy of Knoxville *News Sentinel* and Beck Cultural Exchange Center.)

This photograph shows a young lady being carried to the wagon by patrolman James Rowan, who said he could not be a party to "dragging" the protesters. In 1963, there were still Knoxville laws on the books that kept blacks and whites from mingling at nightclubs downtown. A young Avon Rollins is pictured at left. Rollins serves today as the executive director of the Beck Cultural Exchange Center. (Courtesy of Knoxville *News Sentinel* and Beck Cultural Exchange Center.)

There was resistance to the civil rights movement in Knoxville. This is a photograph of white protesters proclaiming that "Sit-down Demonstrations are Un-American." The counter protesters were from one of the nearby counties and voiced their opinion downtown with a large sign. (Courtesy of Knoxville *News Sentinel* and Beck Cultural Exchange Center.)

Fr. Matthew A. Jones was a spark plug of the civil rights movement in Knoxville. Priest of St. Luke's Episcopal Church, Father Jones was an ardent participant of the movement. Here he marches downtown. (Courtesy of Knoxville *News Sentinel* and Beck Cultural Exchange Center.)

Civil rights marchers were creative in bringing the message home about equal rights. The center sign refers to the "Vertical Plan." As long as black customers stood up to buy something except shoes, there was no problem. Sitting at a lunch counter, however, always caused a "horizontal problem." (Courtesy of Knoxville *News Sentinel* and Beck Cultural Exchange Center.)

This protest was aimed at downtown drugstores. An unidentified man (left) and Jack LeFlore decry the fact that downtown drugstores sold medicines but no sit-down food to blacks. (Courtesy of Knoxville *News Sentinel* and Beck Cultural Exchange Center.)

After mass meetings at a church to bring everybody up to date with what merchants were doing to bring about desegregation, both black and white residents of the community got involved in the movement. Dr. Merrill C. Proudfoot, author of *Diary of a Sit-in*, is fourth from the left. (Courtesy of Knoxville *News Sentinel* and Beck Cultural Exchange Center.)

This 1963 photograph shows a theater employee who tried to stop a Knoxville College student from entering the theater because a group of University of Tennessee students were present. (Courtesy of Knoxville *News Sentinel* and Beck Cultural Exchange Center.)

This is an image of downtown Knoxville around 1963 from the civil rights collection at the Beck Cultural Exchange Center. Policemen were on duty primarily to thwart troublemakers, but they also arrested protesters who refused to obey a command. Sometimes 50 or more people were arrested at a time. (Courtesy of Knoxville *News Sentinel* and Beck Cultural Exchange Center.)

This photograph was taken June 29, 1960, and shows a white man and a black man supporting equal treatment of all people in downtown Knoxville. (Courtesy of Knoxville *News Sentinel* and Beck Cultural Exchange Center.)

This was a nighttime protest at the popular Tennessee Theater, viewed from across the street with a car passing. This 1961 photograph shows a protest of the theater's policies toward blacks in the city. (Courtesy of Knoxville *News Sentinel* and Beck Cultural Exchange Center.)

Rich's Department Store was a focal point for demonstrators. With its fine lunch counter and the plush Laurel Room for dining, Rich's was a prime target for the demonstrators because while blacks were allowed to shop in the store, they were not allowed to eat. (Courtesy of Knoxville *News Sentinel* and Beck Cultural Exchange Center.)

This protest of Rich's Department Store attracted a crowd to watch. The protests of the department store's policies toward blacks eventually led to changes during the civil rights movement. (Courtesy of Knoxville *News Sentinel* and Beck Cultural Exchange Center.)

Four

The Tellico Excavations

The war in Vietnam, the calls to preserve downtown Knoxville, and the civil rights movement so dominated newspapers and broadcast media that one of the most prominent archaeological excavations in U.S. history slipped through the cracks of news coverage. Very few people knew of the archaeological work being done in the Little Tennessee Valley south of Knoxville, but the knowledge gleaned from it rewrote the history of the southeastern United States.

In 1881, the U.S. Congress appropriated funds to the Bureau of Ethnology at the Smithsonian Institute to study Native American mounds. Director John Wesley Powell appointed Cyrus Thomas to direct the explorations. During a five-year period, Thomas excavated more than 2,000 mounds in 22 states and published his results in 1894 disproving the plethora of theories about "lost races" building the mounds and rightfully attributing them to the American Indian. Thomas, however, did uncover an artifact from one of those in the Little Tennessee Valley at the Bat Creek site that has been a subject of controversy to this day. If nothing else, that artifact—known as the "Bat Creek Stone"—made the land along the Little Tennessee River one of the most archaeologically intriguing sites in the United States.

From 1967 to 1981, the Tellico excavations yielded knowledge of close to 20,000 years of Native American history in the region. The first Europeans of record to enter the Little Tennessee Valley were Spanish explorer Hernando De Soto's party in 1540. An old American Indian trail that led to the valley made it a primary location for early native settlement, and proof uncovered during the excavations clearly illustrated that it also served as a center of trade for thousands of years.

The University of Tennessee's McClung Museum director Jefferson Chapman directed the excavations in the Little Tennessee Valley. When he and the crews peeled back the ground in the region, they unearthed a remarkable undisturbed history that has recently been dated back 20,000 years. His book titled *Tellico Archaeology* is the best-documented source of the amazing artifacts uncovered in the 14-year project—many of which are on permanent display at the McClung Museum.

The Bat Creek Stone has generated controversy since it was first excavated in an undisturbed burial mound in 1889 under the direction of Smithsonian archaeologist Cyrus Thomas. While Thomas thought it to be ancient Cherokee, Semitic languages scholar Cyrus Gordon stated in 1971 the inscription is Semitic and specifically Paleo-Hebrew of the first or second century A.D. Many scholars, however, consider the stone artifact to be a fraud, but it did spark archaeological interest in the Little Tennessee Valley. (Courtesy of the Smithsonian Institute.)

One of the most noted European structures in the Tellico project was the French and Indian War's Fort Loudoun, which was built by the British in 1756 to win allies among the Overhill Cherokee. This is a photograph of the present-day Fort Loudoun State Historical Site in Vonore, Tennessee. The fort is a popular destination for natives and visitors to East Tennessee. (Courtesy of the McClung Museum.)

Prior to flooding the region, archaeologists excavated the site, which had long been known to them but never properly studied until the archaeological excavations of the 1960s and 1970s. The digs created a better understanding of the fort and its impact on the Little Tennessee Valley. (Courtesy of the McClung Museum.)

Before the region was overtaken by water, the Fort Loudoun site was raised to preserve the original ground underneath it. The fort is regarded as the oldest European structure west of the Appalachian Mountains. (Courtesy of the McClung Museum.)

This is a line drawing of Fort Loudoun as it appeared in the 1750s. The fort was reconstructed and became a Tennessee state park. The fort is now one of the most popular tourist attractions in the region and holds period-living history weekends where reenactors try to approximate what life was like in the British army in the 18th century. (Courtesy of the McClung Museum.)

This is the excavation at the Tellico Blockhouse. The fortified structure was built to protect the Cherokee from invasive settlers. Future king Louis Philippe of France visited the post in 1799 and observed that the Cherokees "continually supply Tellico with game, eggs, fruits in season, etc. so that the Tellico market is always well stocked, and is certainly one of the best forts in the region." The Blockhouse today is part of the Fort Loudoun Historical Site. (Courtesy of the McClung Museum.)

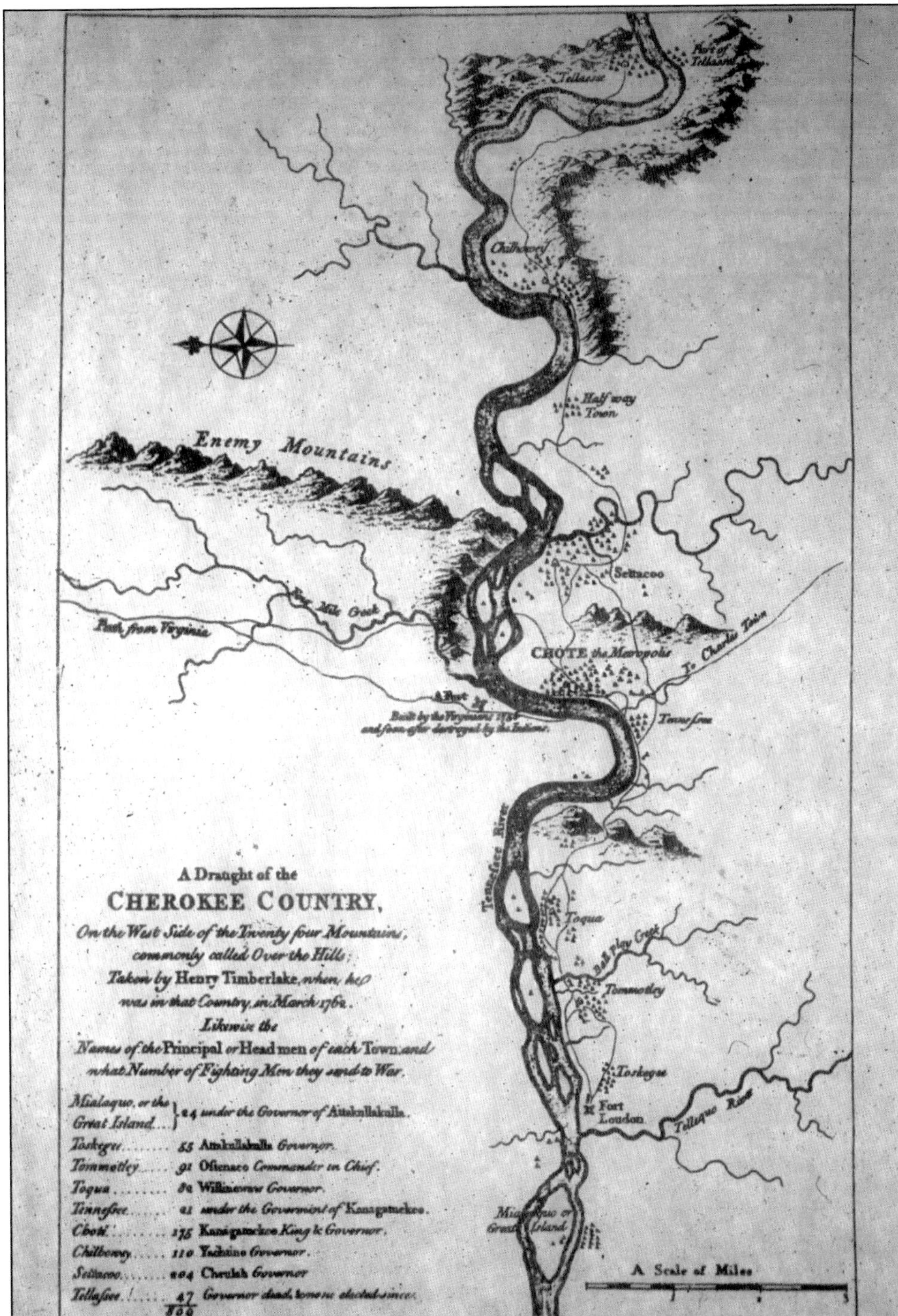

This is the Henry Timberlake map of 1762 that shows the Cherokee villages along the Little Tennessee River. It was an extensive survey of the region and marked the first time the word "Tennessee" was used, which eventually became the name of the state. (Courtesy of the McClung Museum.)

This is an image taken from above of the remains of the Chota Council House showing two people standing at the central hearth of the structure. The aerial view allowed archaeologists to study the ground site and get a better perception of where work needed to begin. (Courtesy of the McClung Museum.)

University of Tennessee students participated in the archaeological excavations of the Tellico region. This photograph shows them assisting in the excavation of Chota. For the Cherokee, this is their ancient capitol and a significant site in their history. It is now under the purview of the Cherokee Nation and part of the Sequoyah Birthplace Museum in Monroe County. (Courtesy of the McClung Museum.)

This is an image of the Tomotley Townhouse and summer pavilion excavation site prior to flooding. Tomotley was reportedly founded around 1750 by Cherokee seeking sanctuary from raids by Creek warriors. The town was razed by the 1776 Virginia expedition and never rebuilt. (Courtesy of McClung Museum.)

A backhoe with a toothless bucket exposes a burial campsite that was dated to 2000 BC. Machinery such as this is specifically designed to uncover archaeological sites with the least amount of damage possible. (Courtesy of the McClung Museum.)

This is a water-screening machine used by archaeologists to sift soil and recover small artifacts. Below, two students sift through the remains from fine-screen material looking for artifacts hidden in the soil. While the work may seem laborious and tedious, this is where some of the greatest finds are discovered in archaeological excavations. (Courtesy of the McClung Museum.)

Here two people map exposed feature and postholes at a Cherokee site. Among the towns excavated and located before flooding was Tanasi—the Cherokee village noted for lending its name to Henry Timberlake's map. A state historical marker near the site proclaims it as the city from which the state of Tennessee got its name. (Courtesy of the McClung Museum.)

The mound of earth seen in this image is the late Mississippian "Toqua" mound (1300–1500 AD). Henry Timberlake's 1762 map showed 32 residences and a council house at the site. He noted that 82 warriors resided there, suggesting a total population of 200 to 300 people. When Louis Phillipe toured the region in 1797, he observed that only 10 houses were present at the site, as it was often a target of hostile settlers during the Revolutionary War. (Courtesy of the McClung Museum.)

Here archaeologists use a technique called "trenching." The process lets them do a controlled excavation of the site with minimal harm. During this process, every grain of dirt is examined by archaeologists for fragments of stone, clay, and metals that would indicate the historical settlement of the site. (Courtesy of the McClung Museum.)

This image shows archaeologists excavating Calloway Island on the Little Tennessee River. The postholes and pits were dated to the Woodland Period around 300 BC. Numerous artifacts from the Woodland Period, such as tools and projectile points, were discovered at the site. Buried human and animal remains were also found in the excavations of the island. (Courtesy of the McClung Museum.)

This photograph shows archaeologists working on the prominent "Ice House Bottom" site, which dates from 7500 BC to 600 AD. This was one of the most exciting excavations because it revealed artifacts originating from Western North Carolina and the midwestern United States—indicating residents might have been intermediaries in a trade culture that existed during the Woodland Period. (Courtesy of the McClung Museum.)

This is an excavation of Rose Island. Over the millennia, floodwaters from the Little Tennessee River washed over succeeding campsites and layered them with sand, creating a "layered cake" of prehistorical sites that University of Tennessee archaeologists were able to view through the excavation process. This illustrates an exposed occupation level dated to around 6500 BC. (Courtesy of the McClung Museum.)

For many archaeologists and scholars of the Archaic and Woodland Periods in the United States, this was one of the greatest finds in the Tellico Archaeology project. If you look closely, you can see the impressions on the clay hearth, indicating a textile-weaving pattern. It has been dated to 7400 BC, but archaeologists studying the artifact have determined it could be as much as 12,000 years old. This find, as well as the other artifacts recovered in the Tellico Archaeology project, gained international prominence—making the McClung Museum and its director, Jefferson Chapman, one of the nation's leading resources on early Native American history. (Courtesy of the McClung Museum.)

Five

THE TENNESSEE RANGER COMPANY

The military program at the University of Tennessee, Knoxville, is older than any other state university in the nation. Prof. Albert Miller Lea—a U.S. Military Academy graduate, introduced it at UT in 1844. Lea organized an infantry company, and from that year forward, the University of Tennessee's Military Science and Leadership program has been regarded as one of the best in the nation.

In 1961, Capt. John S. Daniel was assigned to the university's Reserved Officers Training Corps (ROTC) duty. The Virginia Military Institute alum had received his commission in college and served as a Ranger instructor at the Ranger Camp in Florida. When ordered to report for duty at UT, Daniel came with a plan. He had heard that fellow captains Tony Herbert and Jim Bramlett had started a Ranger training program at his old alma mater, and he decided to try and establish one at UT. With a nod from his commanding officer at the university, Daniel approached the vice president for student affairs, Dr. Herman Spivey, and presented his idea. Spivey gave him approval but no extra funding for the program.

Daniel persevered, and in the fall of 1962, the University of Tennessee became the first ROTC Ranger Training Program to be established at a non-military institution in the United States. It was a rigorous academic and physical program that earned the respect of both civilian and military institutions. The Rangers' black beret became a symbol of honor at UT—even during the anti-war movement that swept the nation's college campuses in the Vietnam War era. On more than one occasion, off-duty cadets found themselves "circling the wagons" around the flagpole to keep protestors from desecrating the flag.

The Tennessee Ranger Company also became a local fixture for the community where they were a regular part of Knoxville's annual Tennessee Agricultural and Industrial Fair, giving demonstrations on their scaling wall for spectators and children. Its greatest legacy, however, was the soldiers it produced—including Capt. Jack Daniel, who would barely survive his tours in Vietnam, rise through the ranks to become a colonel, and be introduced into the U.S. Army's Ranger Hall of Fame. With all of the honors and medals he earned in his distinguished career, Col. Jack Daniel, USA, retired, regards his founding of the UT Army Ranger Program as his greatest achievement.

Capt. John S. Daniel (left), founder of the UT Army Ranger Program, shakes hands with a fellow soldier. During a combat tour in Vietnam, Daniel was badly wounded and told he would never recover completely. Following the physical training program he established at UT, however, Daniel not only recovered from his injuries, but also returned to Vietnam for another tour of duty. (Courtesy of the University of Tennessee Department of Military Science and Leadership.)

This is the plaque the Tennessee Rangers presented to Daniel in 1964. The phrase on top of the award was the motto he came up with for the Tennessee Rangers. As part of the ROTC program at UT, being in the Rangers brought no special privilege and required each cadet to maintain a satisfactory grade point average to remain in the program. (Courtesy of the University of Tennessee Department of Military Science and Leadership.)

When Capt. John S. Daniel received approval to form the UT Ranger Company, he had to locate a number of highly qualified assistants. Sergeant First Class (SFC) Bryan Hall Jackson, seen here erecting a pup tent, was one of those who volunteered to help the program. (Courtesy of the University of Tennessee Department of Military Science and Leadership.)

Another man chosen to help with the Ranger program was former U.S. Marine Corps staff sergeant Harold Long (right). He was a seventh-degree Dan black belt in Isshinryu karate and, at the time, the highest-ranked Caucasian in that particular discipline. He taught hand-to-hand combat skills and would go on to found the Harold Long School of Karate in Knoxville. (Courtesy of the University of Tennessee Department of Military Science and Leadership.)

Pictured above is the first Ranger class at the University of Tennessee in the fall of 1962. This was their first day of physical training as part of the program. Below, the men get instruction at an outdoor training class. The Smoky Mountains and surrounding countryside in Knoxville provided an ideal environment for the Rangers to sharpen their survival skills. (Courtesy of the University of Tennessee Department of Military Science and Leadership.)

The UT Rangers Company marches in the 1962 Veterans Day Parade in downtown Knoxville. One of the mainstays of the cadet program was instilling a sense of community pride and public service. (Courtesy of the University of Tennessee Department of Military Science and Leadership.)

This is the Ranger Volunteer Guard at Castle Heights practicing prior to going to a state drill meet in Nashville. The Volunteer Guard often placed in the top three at the annual Vanderbilt University competition. (Courtesy of the University of Tennessee Department of Military Science and Leadership.)

This is a 1960s-era photograph of classroom-training cadets at the University of Tennessee Army ROTC. In that era, ROTC training was compulsory for those attending UT. When the requirement was eventually dropped, the program continued to grow dramatically. (Courtesy of the University of Tennessee Department of Military Science and Leadership.)

In this class, cadets learn how to operate a PRC-6 military radio. The AN/PRC-6 is a miniature, low-power, battery-operated radio receiver and transmitter designed for communication over short distances. Much of the equipment used in cadet and Ranger training was borrowed from U.S. National Guard and military bases that had it to spare. (Courtesy of the University of Tennessee Department of Military Science and Leadership.)

This is a shot of cadets in headgear watching training films required by the course. In addition to the ROTC and Ranger programs, cadets were expected to carry a full class load and maintain a suitable GPA to allow them to participate in the extracurricular program. (Courtesy of the University of Tennessee Department of Military Science and Leadership.)

Rangers are at attention in this spring 1965 photograph. Program founder Capt. John S. Daniel is on the far left. The young lady in front was a member of the ROTC Auxiliary Corps, which played a major role in the program through fund-raising. (Courtesy of the University of Tennessee Department of Military Science and Leadership.)

This is a photograph of Ranger Cadet Harry G. Hodges (right) saluting his commanding officer. The young cadet would later join the U.S. Navy. Seaman Harry G. Hodges was the first Tennessee Ranger to be killed in action. He was in Da Nang, Vietnam, in 1966 when he came under enemy fire and covered a grenade to save the life of his fellow sentry. For his actions under fire, Hodges was posthumously awarded a Silver Star. (Courtesy of the University of Tennessee Department of Military Science and Leadership.)

While the U.S. Navy provided an attachment for Seaman Hodges, the Tennessee Ranger Company provided the honor guard. Capt. John Daniel (pictured center, right) helps carry the coffin of his former student. (Courtesy of the University of Tennessee Department of Military Science and Leadership.)

A young couple walks through the Arch of Sabers at the University of Tennessee's annual military ball. The annual event was one cadets looked forward to each year. (Courtesy of the University of Tennessee Department of Military Science and Leadership.)

Ranger Cadet training took place at numerous locations throughout the Knoxville area. This is a photograph taken at one of the local farms where the cadets would bivouac. (Courtesy of the University of Tennessee Department of Military Science and Leadership.)

This photograph was taken in April 1964 and shows Capt. John Daniel (at right looking back) and his cadets training in the field. The monthly exercises allowed the cadets to put what they learned in the classroom to practical use and were an integral part of the program. (Courtesy of the University of Tennessee Department of Military Science and Leadership.)

The UT Army Ranger Program lowers the colors. Military protocol was followed at all times while cadets were in uniform. Raising and lowering the flag was a daily ceremony observed by the program. (Courtesy of the University of Tennessee Department of Military Science and Leadership.)

UT Army ROTC commander Col. William Slayden (left) congratulates distinguished military cadets during a ceremony. Because of the mental and physical demands necessary to be a Ranger, Capt. John Daniel had established the Boy Scout method of achievement as a standard, which is still followed to this day. (Courtesy of the University of Tennessee Department of Military Science and Leadership.)

The Volunteer Guard commander cadet Capt. Robert Colvin and sponsor Charlotte Richardson lead the guard in the annual Veterans Day Parade. (Courtesy of the University of Tennessee Department of Military Science and Leadership.)

Colonel Thrasher (right) inspects the Tennessee Rangers in the ranks. It was also common for visiting officers and military dignitaries to inspect the cadets on their tour of the university. (Courtesy of the University of Tennessee Department of Military Science and Leadership.)

Ranger field exercises often pitted locals, who, with the permission of the ROTC instructors, would volunteer to form their own units and engage the Tennessee Rangers as subversives. The exercises were fun for the locals and good training for the cadets. (Courtesy of the University of Tennessee Department of Military Science and Leadership.)

Once a cadet had passed a rigorous examination by a board of ROTC instructors and completed the training necessary, they would be presented the coveted black beret of a U.S. Army Ranger. This photograph is of a beret presentation ceremony in the 1960s. (Courtesy of the University of Tennessee Department of Military Science and Leadership.)

Cadets were trained in Ranger style to operate as a small unit. Here cadet Ron Coulter and two fellow cadets take aim at the enemy during field exercises. (Courtesy of the University of Tennessee Department of Military Science and Leadership.)

This is a photograph of the University of Tennessee U.S. Army ROTC Honor Guard. The five-man squad was selected from a field of candidates and chosen for their abilities to carry and present the colors during football games and other university events. (Courtesy of the University of Tennessee Department of Military Science and Leadership.)

The UT ROTC Color Guard uniforms are on display at the University of Tennessee. The exhibit tells that the uniforms worn by the color guard are replicas of the dragoon uniforms worn by a Knoxville cavalry unit in the Mexican War. (Courtesy of the University of Tennessee Department of Military Science and Leadership.)

Colonel Thrasher pulls inspection of an Army Ranger display. On the right looking down is cadet Harry G. Hodges. At right is cadet Steven G. Ramsey. Ramsey would later be killed in action in Vietnam. In addition, the UT Army Ranger Cadets Charles Ayres, John Tracy, Timothy Worth, and Samuel Asher lost their lives in the Vietnam War. (Courtesy of the University of Tennessee Department of Military Science and Leadership.)

In honor of Seaman Harry G. Hodges, a scholarship fund was set up in his name. Cadet Capt. Joseph Kopecky was the first recipient of the $120 scholarship, which was presented to him at a ceremony the same year. (Courtesy of the University of Tennessee Department of Military Science and Leadership.)

The UT Ranger Company is on parade at an on-campus ceremony. This was awards day in the spring of 1967. Cadet Bill Henry carries the guidon as the company passes in review. (Courtesy of the University of Tennessee Department of Military Science and Leadership.)

A cadet in the Tennessee Army Ranger Company rappels down the side of a cliff during field exercises. Mountaineering was one of the most popular activities for cadets of the Tennessee Ranger Company. (Courtesy of the University of Tennessee Department of Military Science and Leadership.)

Mountaineering, land navigation, and reconnaissance training were all included in the field exercises of the program. Here a Ranger goes hand over hand across a stream in East Tennessee. (Courtesy of the University of Tennessee Department of Military Science and Leadership.)

This 1968 photograph of "Griz's Guerilla's" was taken at the University of Tennessee Farm off of Alcoa Highway. From left to right, cadets ? Griswold, Carson Blackburn, ? Anderson, ? Boyatt, Phelan, ? Henry, ? Vance, ? Asher, and ? Higgs take time to pose during training. (Courtesy of the University of Tennessee Department of Military Science and Leadership.)

This is a photograph of Ranger Company commander Rob Key on the wall at the Tennessee Valley Agricultural and Industrial (TVA&I) Fair. The UT Army Rangers placed this wall on the fairgrounds and gave regular demonstrations during the annual event. It is the first image most East Tennessee children have of the Army Ranger Program at the university. (Courtesy of the University of Tennessee Department of Military Science and Leadership.)

In addition to scaling and rappelling down the wall, cadets of the Army Ranger program would also do demonstrations of hand-to-hand combat and lectures on the U.S. Army Rangers. Regional school groups always made the Ranger Wall an educational stop on their visits to the fair. The Tennessee Ranger program still exists and is one of the most popular programs in UT's Department of Military Science and Leadership. (Courtesy of the University of Tennessee Department of Military Science and Leadership.)

This photograph of the UT ROTC leadership was taken in the early 1970s. At left is Morristown native UT Army Ranger commander Gary D. Birchfield. Standing next to him is company commander Randolph Duffy of Knoxville. (Courtesy of the University of Tennessee Department of Military Science and Leadership.)

Col. John F. Reed congratulates and presents a corsage to D Company sponsor Joyce Bryant at Neyland Stadium. The women's UT ROTC sponsor corps was a driving force in the entire program. They volunteered their time and effort to aiding and assisting the university program and veterans at home and abroad. (Courtesy of the University of Tennessee Department of Military Science and Leadership.)

The UT ROTC Sponsor Corps visited Washington, D.C. While many were girlfriends of the cadets, a good number were unaffiliated and simply enjoyed being part of the program. This is a photograph of the Sponsor Corps standing on the steps of the capitol with former Knoxville mayor and then-U.S. representative John J. Duncan Sr. (Courtesy of the University of Tennessee Department of Military Science and Leadership.)

The UT ROTC Army Sponsor Corps gathers for a photograph outside the dormitories of the university. (Courtesy of the University of Tennessee Department of Military Science and Leadership.)

The UT ROTC Sponsor Corps visits returning Vietnam War veterans at Walter Reed Hospital in Washington, D.C. Sponsor Corps members take time to offer a kind word and talk to the veterans. Below, two Sponsor Corps volunteers take a veteran for a spin in his wheelchair. (Courtesy of the University of Tennessee Department of Military Science and Leadership.)

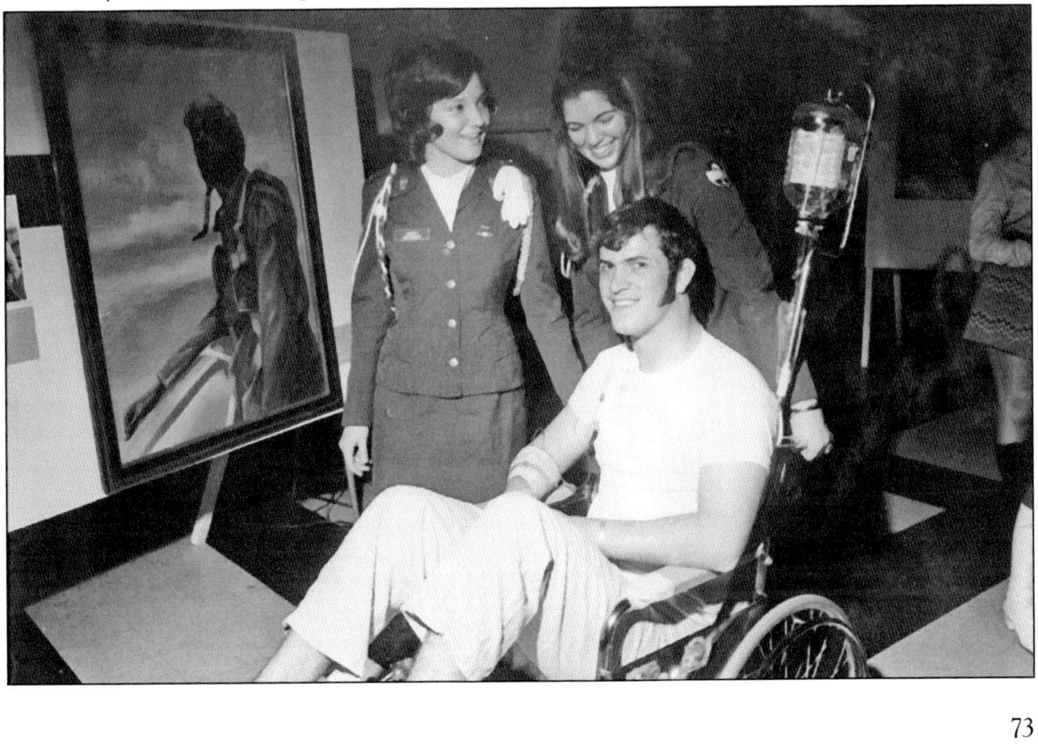

The UT ROTC Sponsor Corps were guests at a tea held in Washington, D.C., by Katherine "Kitsy" Westmoreland (far right)—the wife of Spartanburg native Gen. William C. Westmoreland, who commanded American military operations in the Vietnam War at its peak from 1964 to 1968 and who later served as the U.S. Army Chief of Staff from 1968 to 1972. Below, three Sponsor Corps members take time to sample the tea and relax. (Courtesy of the University of Tennessee Department of Military Science and Leadership.)

Kitsy Westmoreland (left) takes time to talk to the women of the UT ROTC Sponsor Corps and an unidentified male chaperone for the group. The Sponsor Corps' work in D.C. was recognized as a much-needed show of support for the men and women in uniform in the Vietnam War. Below, two women of the corps talk to a gentleman during the tea party, which was also attended by dignitaries and military personnel from Washington, D.C. (Courtesy of the University of Tennessee Department of Military Science and Leadership.)

One of the many ways the UT ROTC Sponsor Corps assisted the program was by working as ushers and volunteering to raise awareness of the ROTC program and former classmates serving in Vietnam. Here members of the Sponsor Corps get the opportunity to meet country music entertainer Johnny Cash and his wife, June Carter Cash, backstage in Knoxville, where they pose for a picture with the legendary singer. (Courtesy of the University of Tennessee Department of Military Science and Leadership.)

UT ROTC Sponsor Corps member Brenda Naper fills her autograph collection with signatures from Johnny and June Carter Cash. The Sponsor Corps program eventually ended at the University of Tennessee, and there is some talk about reactivating the group. What the organization did in fund-raising for the cadet programs and their work with veterans was recognized on numerous occasions on both a local and national level. They were a friendly voice in a storm for young men shipping over to or returning from the battlefields of Vietnam. (Courtesy of the University of Tennessee Department of Military Science and Leadership.)

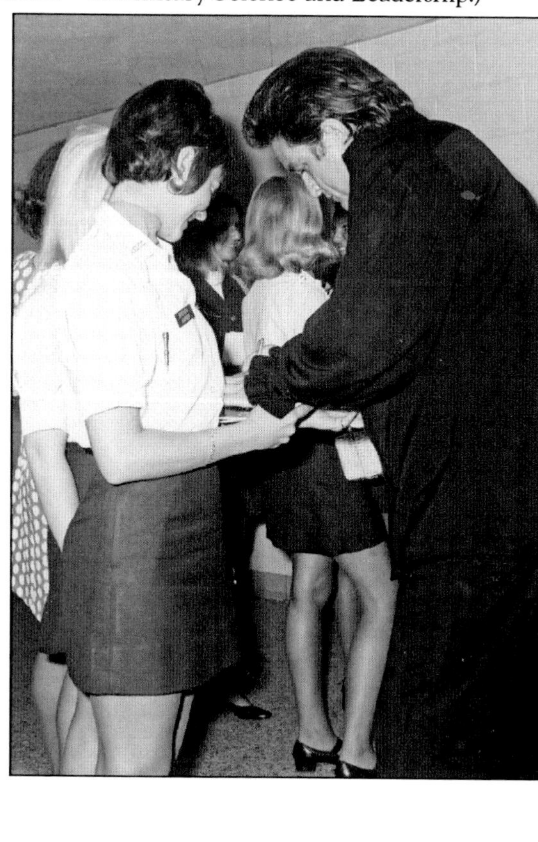

Six

Medal of Honor Recipient Sgt. Mitchell Stout

Mitchell William Stout was your average local kid. He was born at St. Mary's Hospital on February 24, 1950, and spent his childhood growing up in the Dixie Lee Junction area of West Knox County. His mother worked as a nurse for Parkwest Hospital. When he was still young, Mitchell's parents divorced, and he lived with his mother, Faye. He attended Highland Park Elementary in Loudon County and went on to attend Lenoir City High School.

He quit Lenoir City High School his senior year and started bouncing around trying to figure out what to do with his life. He went to see his father, Jack Stout, who had been transferred to Sanford, North Carolina. While staying with him, Mitchell decided to volunteer for the U.S. Army. His mother did not approve of it really but knew once her son made up his mind there was little she could do.

During his first tour of duty, Pvt. Mitchell Stout distinguished himself as a soldier and proved himself under fire on numerous occasions—earning a Bronze Star and the rank of sergeant. The "Dusters" he was assigned to (light, armored military vehicles) saw some of the hardest action in Vietnam and were often the target of choice in most North Vietnamese attacks.

After a visit home with his mother, Faye Thomas, Stout returned for a second tour of duty and was assigned to Battery C, 1st Battalion, 44th Artillery Unit and posted at a base defending Khe Gio Bridge—a field base located 15 miles west of battalion headquarters. He was one of 14 Americans on the post, which was also supported by more than 50 South Vietnamese soldiers. On the night of March 11, 1970, they came under heavy attack. In the heat of the battle, he noticed a North Vietnam army grenade in the bunker where he and the men had taken cover. Without a thought, he grabbed it off the floor, made it to the doorway, and used his body to absorb the blast. For his actions under fire, Sgt. Mitchell William Stout became the first serviceman in the history of the army's 1st Battalion to be awarded the Medal of Honor.

This is a photograph taken of Mitchell Stout before he left for Vietnam. From left to right are Kenny Dyer, Steve Kelly, William Fanning, and Mitchell Stout. Stout dropped out of school and was visiting his father in North Carolina when he decided to join the army. (Courtesy of Faye Thomas.)

During his first tour of duty, Stout got to know Vietnam and its people. Here he takes a moment to go for a swim. Stout spent a great deal of time growing up in rural Knox and Loudon Counties and could reportedly make himself at home in Vietnam. (Courtesy of Faye Thomas.)

Mitchell Stout (right) relaxes with a couple of friends and a 45-rpm record player. Stout told his mother he had come to like Vietnam and the men with which he served. He felt that going back would let him teach others how to survive their tours of duty. (Courtesy of Faye Thomas.)

This is Mitchell Stout standing next to a Duster. Of the Duster units in the Vietnam War, Hugh Roberts, former president of the Dusters, Quads, and Searchlights Association, said, "We were the most highly decorated army artillery outfit in Vietnam and the only Air Defense Artillery unit with a Congressional Medal of Honor recipient—Mitchell Stout. We were awarded Presidential and Meritorious Unit citations, Silver Stars, Bronze stars, and over 1,000 Purple Hearts. . . Over four million 40 MM rounds, ten million .50 cal. rounds, and a million miles of illumination from the D.M.Z. (demilitarized zone) to the Delta." (Courtesy of Faye Thomas.)

This is a family photograph taken during the holidays in 1969 with Mitchell Stout and his mother, Faye Thomas. It was during this holiday trip home, however, that Mitchell informed his mother he was volunteering for a second tour of duty in Vietnam. (Courtesy of Faye Thomas.)

This was a light-hearted photograph Mitchell Stout sent home to his mother from the front lines in Vietnam. On the back of the photograph are the words, "Beer break, Love, Mitchell." Stout's mother said her son genuinely enjoyed his time in the army and the friends he made while he was there. (Courtesy of Faye Thomas.)

This is one of the last photographs Mitchell Stout sent home to his mother. He is standing at his post at Khe Gio Bridge. The U.S. Army outpost was located on Highway 9 near the DMZ that separated North and South Vietnam. Of the 14 Americans who fought in this battle, two were killed, five wounded, and one captured. The ARVN garrison had six dead and nine wounded. The North Vietnamese army lost about 40 men in the attack. (Courtesy of Faye Thomas.)

This is one of the first images Mitchell Stout sent home from Vietnam. Mitchell Stout's memory faded as time went by, but childhood friend James R. "Buddy" White made sure no one forgot the Knoxville native. He erected a monument at Virtue Cemetery in Knoxville commemorating Stout and was an active participant in seeing that all Medal of Honor recipients from Tennessee were properly honored. While Stout was born and raised in Knoxville, his entrance into the army in North Carolina has him officially credited to that state. (Courtesy of Faye Thomas.)

The President of the United States
in the name of Congress
takes pleasure in presenting the

Medal of Honor

to

MITCHELL W. STOUT

Rank and organization: Sergeant, U.S. Army, Battery C, 1st Battalion, 44th Artillery
Place and Date: Khe Gio Bridge, Republic of Vietnam, 12 March 1970
Entered service: Raleigh, North Carolina
Born: 24 February 1950, Knoxville, Tennessee

Citation:
Sgt. Stout distinguished himself during an attack by a North Vietnamese Army Sapper company on his unit's firing position at Khe Gio Bridge. Sgt. Stout was in a bunker with members of a searchlight crew when the position came under heavy enemy mortar fire and ground attack. When the intensity of the mortar attack subsided, an enemy grenade was thrown into the bunker. Displaying great courage, Sgt. Stout ran to the grenade, picked it up, and started out of the bunker. As he reached the door, the grenade exploded. By holding the grenade close to his body and shielding its blast, he protected his fellow soldiers in the bunker from further injury or death. Sgt. Stout's conspicuous gallantry and intrepidity in action, at the cost of his own life, are in keeping with the highest traditions of the military service and reflect great credit upon him, his unit and the U.S. Army.

National Medal of Honor Museum of Military History, Chattanooga, Tennessee

This is the Medal of Honor citation posthumously presented when Sgt. Mitchell Stout, USA, was awarded the nation's highest military honor. (Courtesy of the National Medal of Honor Museum of Military History.)

Seven

The Soldiers of Vietnam

The faces of U.S. servicemen who stare back from the deltas, jungles, and battlefields of Vietnam speak volumes about the hardships of the war they were ordered to fight. They were the usual faces of war—young men and women from all walks of life. It did not matter if they were drafted or volunteered. They answered their nation's call to duty, performed valiantly, and completed their missions, but they returned home to a nation tired of war and tired of them.

Fortunately, protests and anti-military sentiments in East Tennessee were largely confined to college campuses and never really ventured too far away from them. Newspaper photographers and camera crews, however, always seemed to find them, and their stories of civil disobedience and disruption eclipsed those of the soldiers on the battlefields and in the jungles of Vietnam. It was a time of social upheaval in the United States that did not go unnoticed on the battlefields more than 9,000 miles away, but the changes were far more radical than they realized.

Unlike their fathers in wars past, the Vietnam veterans' historical stories of individual accomplishment and courage under fire were not deemed worthy enough to record or preserve. Some of the greatest stories of leadership and American warrior achievement happened in the Vietnam War, but there was no incentive for the soldiers to tell them and those who tried were shouted down or disregarded. The civilian leadership and armchair diplomats who sent Americans to an unpopular war and directed its course for 15 years did not bear the burden of failure in the nation's eyes. The blame was wrongly assigned to the veterans who served, and these men and women—an entire generation—were robbed of their accomplishments and heroes.

Even Knoxville, with its longstanding military tradition, was not unaffected by the headlines and nightly news broadcasts of the anti-military movement in America. There were no welcome home celebrations or acknowledgments of a job well done. In fact, for many it was quite the opposite, and so most just faded into the background of American society—harboring the memories, pains, and stories of a war everyone wanted to forget. Only now are some of these veterans willing to tell their stories and share that part of their life. These are the photographs and the memories of Vietnam as seen through the eyes of those who served.

This is New Market, Tennessee, native Max Stiner. He served as an infantryman in Vietnam during 1968–1969, serving during a period of time when the war was escalating in South Vietnam. He was sent to a base in the Tay Ninh Province. The region was a hotbed for North Vietnamese and Viet Cong activity. (Courtesy of C. L. Brown.)

This photograph shows Stiner playing horseshoes at a base in Suoi Da, Vietnam, with anyone who would challenge the East Tennessean. It was a game Stiner had played throughout his youth, and he was practically unbeatable, which more than one person found out during his tour of duty. (Courtesy of C. L. Brown.)

Max Stiner served during the massive Tet Offensive. The offensive covered the entire nation of Vietnam, involving around 80,000 Communist troops who attacked more than 100 towns and cities, including 36 of 44 provincial capitals, 5 cities, 72 district towns, and Saigon. The offensive was one of the largest military operations ever conducted by either side. (Courtesy of C. L. Brown.)

Max Stiner and company are stretching the skin of a tiger in December 1968. The tiger found its way near the perimeter, and the men were forced to shoot it as it posed a hazard. The animal was seven feet, seven inches long and weighed more than 290 pounds. (Courtesy of C. L. Brown.)

This is a photograph of Sgt. Tom Jones (left) and Larry Helton of Georgia making a stream crossing in Vietnam. They were members of the 196th Light Infantry serving in the Tay Ninh Province. (Courtesy of Tommy Jones.)

Jones and his company get a ride on an armored personnel carrier. The men would often ride on top of the vehicle to protect themselves from explosive mines that could detonate under it. (Courtesy of Tommy Jones.)

The Boeing Chinook was a workhorse in the Vietnam War capable of carrying large loads of troops and cargo. Below is a photograph of a Chinook lifting a load of cargo off the deck. There was a wide loading ramp at the rear of the fuselage and three external cargo hooks. Its primary role was troop movement, artillery emplacement, and battlefield resupply. (Courtesy of Tommy Jones.)

This is an image of Tommy Jones (left) and Larry Helton holding their M60. The men were part of the light infantry division's machine gun squads, which often bore the brunt of enemy attacks. Because of their small numbers and deadly effect, the light infantry division was often called upon to relieve forces that were pinned down. (Courtesy of Tommy Jones.)

This off-center photograph was taken on patrol in the jungles of the Tay Ninh Province. The region developed into a major action area after a large enemy base camp was uncovered there in October 1966. (Courtesy of Tommy Jones.)

Sgt. Tommy Jones (third from left) stands for a group shot with his platoon leader and South Korean soldiers at the Chu Lai Base. Chu Lai served as a base of operations for thousands of troops in the Vietnam War. (Courtesy of Tommy Jones.)

Sgt. Tommy Jones (left) stands with a friend holding an M16 at Monkey Park near Chu Lai. Jones spent six months in the 196th LID and six months in the Americal Division, which the division merged into on September 25, 1967. (Courtesy of Tommy Jones.)

The rock Jones and his friend were standing in front of commemorates a USO visit to Chu Lai at Monkey Park in July 1967. (Courtesy of Tommy Jones.)

In the background of the photograph, one can see a plume of smoke rise near the perimeter of Chu Lai. The 196th LID saw some of the conflict's heaviest action. Below is a sandbagged bunker protecting the high ground, which gave the soldiers a commanding field of fire should they be attacked. (Courtesy of Tommy Jones.)

This is Sam Parker. He was one of three brothers from Knoxville to serve in Europe during World War II, serving during the Battle of the Bulge and the final Allied push toward Berlin. His son served in Vietnam. (Courtesy of Kathy Jones.)

Jackie Parker is the son of Sam Parker. He was drafted in 1966 and served in the 15th Engineering Battalion of the 9th Infantry Division at Dong Tam, Vietnam. (Courtesy of Jackie Parker.)

A young Jackie Parker hangs on to a chain on the USNS *Sultan* as she takes him to Vietnam. The ship was a major troop carrier during the conflict. The voyage from California to Vietnam took two weeks, and the ship was the principal transport for large numbers of troops to Southeast Asia. (Courtesy of Jackie Parker.)

Parker served in the Mekong Delta where the 9th Infantry Division saw some of the heaviest action in the war. It is the region in southwestern Vietnam where the Mekong River approaches and empties into the sea. It was a favorite hiding place for enemy guerilla forces and the North Vietnamese army. (Courtesy of Jackie Parker.)

Knoxvillian Gary Cooper joined the navy in 1969 and served in the Sea Bees working on projects in Da Nang. In 1972, he joined the U.S. Army. Overall he served three tours in Vietnam. He died in 2005 with the cause of death listed as "exposure to Agent Orange." (Courtesy of Kathy Jones.)

Earl Polson was drafted to Vietnam where he served from September 1966 to September 1997. He served with the 191st Ordnance Battalion. He is standing in front of the building where he worked as a radio operator. (Courtesy of Earl Polson.)

Above is a photograph taken of the 191st Ordnance Battalion aboard the USNS *Geiger*. The troop ships in Vietnam were invaluable to moving large numbers of troops up and down the coast of Vietnam. Below is an image of a troop transport ship disembarking soldiers at Qui Nohn in South Vietnam. (Courtesy of Earl Polson.)

U.S. Air Force sergeant Jim Ware served with the 1876 Communications Squad at Tan Son Nhut Air Force Base in Saigon, Vietnam. When he first arrived in the Vietnamese capital, the war had not ventured near the city. (Courtesy of Jim Ware.)

This is the entrance to Tan Son Nhut Air Force Base in Saigon. Although it was an important secured military facility, base operations often utilized local civilians in maintenance and construction projects. (Courtesy of Jim Ware.)

This pictured shows aircraft kept at Tan Son Nhut Air Force Base. This location is where thousands of American troops were first brought into Vietnam. U.S. Air Force personnel managed air operations for military aircraft coming and going into the Asian nation. (Courtesy of Jim Ware.)

Sgt. Jim Ware took this photograph of a U.S. Army helicopter coming in for a landing. While fixed-wing aircraft were a mainstay in the conflict, Vietnam is remembered as the helicopter war. The maneuverable aircraft was invaluable as an attack vehicle and troop carrier. (Courtesy of Jim Ware.)

Jim Ware snapped this photograph of the 25th Infantry Division convoy preparing to roll into South Vietnam out of the window of his office. The airbase was a vital center of operations for troop movements throughout the Vietnam War. (Courtesy of Jim Ware.)

Vietnamese civilians worked at the air base throughout the war. As enemy action began to creep into Saigon, base security became more endangered. Some locals would work during the day "spotting" or mapping strategic locations and act as enemy guerillas at night. (Courtesy of Jim Ware.)

This is a photograph taken of Sgt. Jim Ware in February 1968 with two South Vietnamese airmen who served with him in the 1876 Communications Squad. Ware would go on to retire from the U.S. Air Force and today sits on the board of directors of the Beck Cultural Exchange Center in Knoxville. (Courtesy of Jim Ware.)

As Saigon became a hot spot for enemy action, base security increased dramatically. Here a residence is sandbagged against enemy attacks. Ware noted they could first walk around Saigon in civilian clothing, but base security eventually dictated uniforms only for military personnel both on base and throughout the city. (Courtesy of Jim Ware.)

James Harrell of Knoxville was drafted to Vietnam and served from July 1969 to December 1970. He served with the 44th Artillery, Battery B, 1st Battalion. (Courtesy of James Harrell.)

Sgt. John Burgess of the U.S. Army's 3rd Battalion, 5th Armored Cavalry, 9th Infantry Division, was drafted into Vietnam and started his tour of duty August 1, 1968. Eight months later, he was in Quang Tri, South Vietnam, when his unit was attacked. During the ensuing battle, he was killed in action. He was posthumously awarded the Silver Star for his actions under fire. (Courtesy of Ray Kinsland of the Cherokee Boys Club.)

Richard Romine of Dandridge served in Vietnam from 1966 to 1968 with the 196th Light Infantry Division. The East Tennessee native served with distinction in Vietnam—proving himself under fire on numerous occasions, including during the Tet Offensive. (Courtesy of Richard Romine.)

Mail call was a rare treat for soldiers in the field. Sergeant Romine, on the right in this photograph, and the men in his company take a break from their duties to read letters from home. Maintaining morale in the ranks was a difficult job. The North Vietnamese army, who followed U.S. news reports more than the Americans in the field, would often use psychological warfare tactics in attempts to demoralize the troops on the ground. (Courtesy of Richard Romine.)

Sgt. Richard Romine (seated in center) and men rest on patrol. During his time in Vietnam, Romine and his men spent a great deal of time patrolling the Ho Chi Minh Trail, where they were attacked numerous times by the North Vietnamese army. In one encounter, he barely escaped with serious wounds to his legs. (Courtesy of Richard Romine.)

Here Sergeant Romine (far right), his friend Marshall (center), and another member of his unit enjoy some rare downtime on an island off of South China Beach. The 196th LID was reassigned to a marine base while the marines took a 30-day R&R leave. (Courtesy of Richard Romine.)

Sgt. Richard Romine was brevetted (field promoted) to the rank of captain following the Battle of Da Nang. Here he is on patrol. During his tour of duty in Vietnam, the 196th LID spent a good deal of time operating along the Cambodia and Laotian border where enemy engagements with both regulars and guerillas happened on a regular basis. (Courtesy of Richard Romine.)

"We spent a lot of time playing with the Vietnamese kids," said Richard Romine. "Most of them would hang around the beaches where there were soldiers, and we always had to be careful because we didn't know who the enemy was." (Courtesy of Richard Romine.)

Sergeant Romine is shown here with his friend Marshall from Lakewood, California. While on patrol, Marshall, who was Romine's machine gunner, was shot and killed during an attack. Romine had become very close with Marshall and wrote often to his family after his death. He personally returned his friend's personal effects to Marshall's parents when he returned stateside. (Courtesy of Richard Romine.)

Sgt. Richard Romine's tour of duty in Vietnam was a decorated one; when he returned home, he held a Bronze Star for courage and leadership under fire and a Purple Heart for the wounds he sustained in battle. He served with the 196th LID for six months and in the Americal Division for the other six months, but his assignments in the front action never changed. Here he gets a chance to rest in a lawn chair on South China Beach Island. (Courtesy of Richard Romine.)

M.Sgt. Mike Keenam was an instructor at the University of Tennessee where he worked with the Tennessee Ranger Company. He would later do a tour of duty in Vietnam and return to head up the Reserved Officers Training Corps (ROTC) at Tennessee Technological University. (Courtesy of University of Tennessee Department of Military Science and Leadership.)

This is a Southeast Asian "chopper storm" coming from Bien Hoa Air Base located near Saigon. Men of the 199th Light Infantry Brigade wait for helicopters to pick them up for transport down range in Vietnam. The helicopter was a primary attack and transport vehicle during the Vietnam War. (Courtesy of Stephen Mitchell.)

Tanks are positioned at 199th LIB base camp at Bien Chanh. The 199th LIB was a highly effective unit in the Vietnam War. Their primary responsibility was to secure the main infiltration routes used by the North Vietnamese army. (Courtesy of Stephen Mitchell.)

Sp4c. Stephen Allen Mitchell of Knoxville (right) was drafted in 1967. He served in 1968 and 1969 with the 199th Light Infantry Brigade. The Knoxvillian participated in numerous engagements with the North Vietnamese and fought in the Tet Offensive of 1968, where the 199th LIB sustained heavy casualties. (Courtesy of Stephen Mitchell.)

Stephen Mitchell takes advantage of some downtime to grab a shave in the field. The 199th LIB stayed in active contact with the enemy throughout his tour in the country, and time to do basic things like shaving provided a boost in morale. (Courtesy of Stephen Mitchell.)

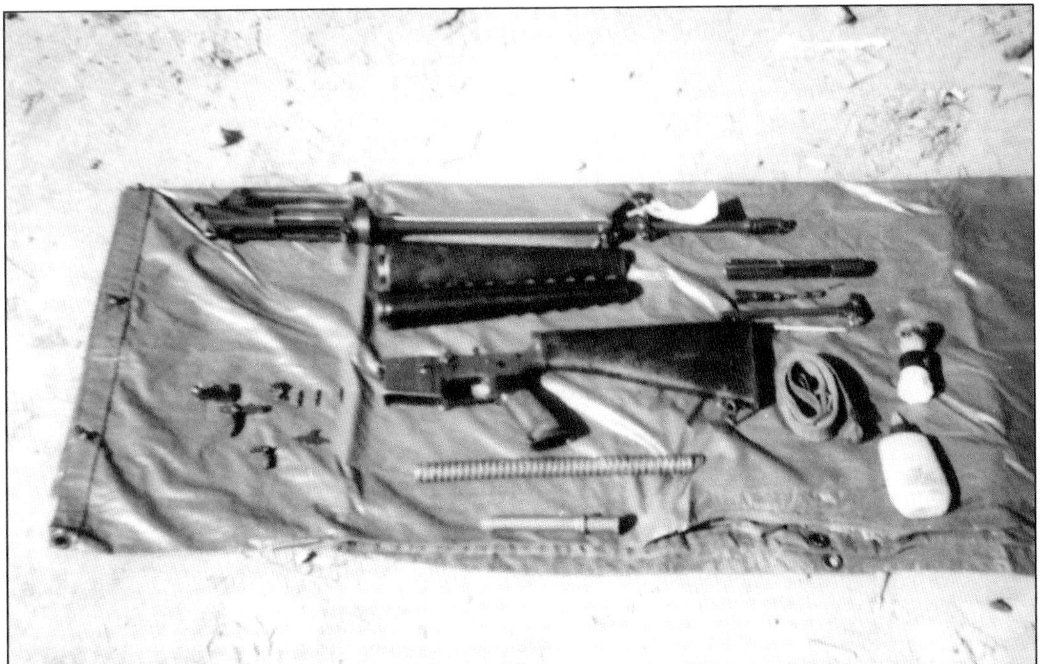

With the mud, sand, and changing weather conditions of Vietnam, maintaining a rifle that your life depended on required daily cleaning. This is a photograph of a standard-issue M16 rifle disassembled and ready for maintenance. (Courtesy of Stephen Mitchell.)

A soldier of the 199th LIB crosses a delta with his rifle above his head. The dense jungles and marshes were filled with nests of North Vietnamese and civilian guerillas. Great caution had to be taken when fording a stream or a river because a soldier was completely vulnerable to attack in the treacherous and disease-filled waters of Vietnam. (Courtesy of Stephen Mitchell.)

Company members cross a marsh in single file. It was at this time that a unit could be trapped by a sniper, who could pin down soldiers and buy enough time for a small force of guerillas to wreak havoc on the unit. (Courtesy of Stephen Mitchell.)

Members of the 199 LIB take a break from building a bunker. Stephen Mitchell and his company spent a great deal of time doing reconnaissance missions to locate enemy forces, which often resulted in engaging enemy forces. (Courtesy of Stephen Mitchell.)

The company pauses for a minute after a day in the mud. Standing from left to right are Russell Greg of Missouri, Randy Pilgrim from Tennessee, Jack Gates from Maryland, and Ron Williams of Kentucky. Squatting with the rifle is Stephen Mitchell. (Courtesy of Stephen Mitchell.)

A dog trainer of the 199th LIB walks a German shepherd across a rice paddy. The dogs were trained to sniff out enemy soldiers, who often hid in the paddies. Americans were forbidden from walking on the dikes between paddies because enemy forces often booby-trapped them with explosive charges. One of the German shepherds spent so long in Vietnam that it actually carried the honorary rank of major. (Courtesy of Stephen Mitchell.)

Stephen Mitchell is the field radio operator taking a look back as he crosses a marsh. The radio operator was one of the most important men on the crew during an enemy attack because they could call in air support or alert other units. (Courtesy of Stephen Mitchell.)

Stephen Mitchell grabs some shuteye in a hammock. Hammocks were oftentimes preferred over sleeping on the ground because of the animals that could come into camp at night. (Courtesy of Stephen Mitchell.)

Mitchell sits atop a bunker guarding the high ground, which was called Signal Mountain. During the Tet Offensive, the 199th LIB were brutally attacked and retaliated with a vengeance, killing more than 500 of the enemy in the first 14 hours of the battle. After three days of sustained attacks by the 275th Viet Cong Regiment, the 199th LIB was credited with more than 900 enemy kills. (Courtesy of Stephen Mitchell.)

Sp4c. Stephen Mitchell pauses for a moment during patrol on his 21st birthday on June 17, 1968. The 199th LIB's special training in counter intelligence and their ability to move quickly under fire made them one of the most decorated units in the Vietnam War with 14 Distinguished Service Crosses and four Medals of Honor awarded for their actions under fire. (Courtesy of Stephen Mitchell.)

A Chinook helicopter lowers freight at a communications installation. Such posts were vital to field units for a variety of reasons, including the ability to call in air support. (Courtesy of Stephen Mitchell.)

This was a rare night for members of the 199th LIB at base camp in Bien Hoa during a "stand-down," where they would resupply, get medical check-ups, and perform maintenance on their weapons. From left to right are (sitting) Sgt. Randall Pilgrim of Jasper, Tennessee, and Sp4c. Stephen Mitchell of Knoxville, Tennessee; (standing) Sp4c. John Christan of Painesville, Ohio; Sp4c. Thomas Scott of Richmond, Virginia; and PFC Gary Schutzle of South Dakota. (Courtesy of Stephen Mitchell.)

This is probably one of the most familiar sights people have of the Vietnam War: a gunship flying over the countryside of South Vietnam taking in troops and supplies to the front. The gunships were a lifeline in the largely rural sections of the nation where North Vietnamese and civilian guerillas often attacked U.S. forces. (Courtesy of Stephen Mitchell.)

This is Sp4c. Stephen Mitchell standing next to a car in Fort Benning, Georgia, where he was sent after his tour in Vietnam to train other troops heading to Southeast Asia. Mitchell resides today in North Knoxville. (Courtesy of Stephen Mitchell.)

To honor the more than 58,000 U.S. servicemen and women killed in action in Vietnam, former 199th Light Infantry Brigade veteran Jan Scruggs of Maryland, who was wounded in action, used the proceeds from a used car he sold to start a memorial fund when Congress refused to help fund it. More than 275,000 individuals—mostly veterans of the war—added to that amount, raising more than $8 million to build the Vietnam Veterans Memorial Wall in Washington, D.C. (Courtesy of Jan Scruggs and the Vietnam Veterans Memorial.)

The Vietnam Veterans Memorial was officially dedicated in 1982 and is located in Constitution Gardens adjacent to the National Mall. Each year, more than three million people visit the memorial. It is unique and marks the first time in U.S. history that the veterans who fought in an American war primarily funded their own national memorial to commemorate their fellow Americans who gave their lives in it. (Courtesy of Jan Scruggs and the Vietnam Veterans Memorial.)

BIBLIOGRAPHY

Chapman, Jefferson. *Tellico Archaeology*. Knoxville, TN: University of Tennessee Press, 2001.
Creekmore, Betsy. *Knox County, Tennessee*. Virginia Beach, VA: Donning Company, 1988.
Deadrick, Lucille. *Heart of the Valley: A History of Knoxville, Tennessee*. Knoxillve, TN: East Tennessee Historical Society, 1976.
Donlon, Roger, MOH. *Beyond Nam Dong*. Leavenworth, KS: R8N Publishers, 1998.
Hooper, William E. *Tennessee Online*, 1996. http://www.tennesseehistory.com.
Jordan, Kenneth N. Sr. *Heroes of Our Time*. Atglen, PA: Schiffer Publishing, 1994.
Rothrock, Mary. *The French Broad-Holston Country*. Knoxville, TN: East Tennessee Historical Society, 1946.

Consistent with our mission to preserve history on a local level, this book was printed in South Carolina on American-made paper and manufactured entirely in the United States. Products carrying the accredited Forest Stewardship Council (FSC) label are printed on 100 percent FSC-certified paper.

MADE IN THE USA